IF FO

👤 _____

✉ _____

📱 _____

Greater Than a Tourist Book Series
Reviews from Readers

I think the series is wonderful and beneficial for tourists to get information before visiting the city.

-Seckin Zumbul, Izmir Turkey

I am a world traveler who has read many trip guides but this one really made a difference for me. I would call it a heartfelt creation of a local guide expert instead of just a guide.

-Susy, Isla Holbox, Mexico

New to the area like me, this is a must have!

 -Joe, Bloomington, USA

This is a good series that gets down to it when looking for things to do at your destination without having to read a novel for just a few ideas.

-Rachel, Monterey, USA

Good information to have to plan my trip to this destination.

-Pennie Farrell, Mexico

Great ideas for a port day.

-Mary Martin USA

Aptly titled, you won't just be a tourist after reading this book. You'll be greater than a tourist!

-Alan Warner, Grand Rapids, USA

Even though I only have three days to spend in San Miguel in an upcoming visit, I will use the author's suggestions to guide some of my time there. An easy read - with chapters named to guide me in directions I want to go.

-Robert Catapano, USA

Great insights from a local perspective! Useful information and a very good value!

-Sarah, USA

This series provides an in-depth experience through the eyes of a local. Reading these series will help you to travel the city in with confidence and it'll make your journey a unique one.

-Andrew Teoh, Ipoh, Malaysia

>TOURIST

GREATER THAN A TOURIST- POZNAN POLAND

50 Travel Tips from a Local

SERKAN DABAN

Greater Than a Tourist- Poznań, Poland Copyright © 2018 by CZYK Publishing LLC. All Rights Reserved.

All rights reserved. No part of this book may be reproduced in any form or by any electronic or mechanical means including information storage and retrieval systems, without permission in writing from the author. The only exception is by a reviewer, who may quote short excerpts in a review.

The statements in this book are of the authors and may not be the views of CZYK Publishing or Greater Than a Tourist.

Cover designed by: Ivana Stamenkovic
Cover Image: https://pixabay.com/en/mikołajki-poznan-in-the-morning-3859826/

CZYK Publishing Since 2011.

Greater Than a Tourist
Visit our website at www.GreaterThanaTourist.com

Lock Haven, PA
All rights reserved.
ISBN: 9781792038716

>TOURIST

50 TRAVEL TIPS FROM A LOCAL

BOOK DESCRIPTION

Are you excited about planning your next trip?

Do you want to try something new?

Would you like some guidance from a local?

If you answered yes to any of these questions, then this Greater Than a Tourist book is for you.

Greater Than a Tourist- Poznań, Poland by Serkan Daban offers the inside scoop on Poznań. Most travel books tell you how to travel like a tourist. Although there is nothing wrong with that, as part of the Greater Than a Tourist series, this book will give you travel tips from someone who has lived at your next travel destination.

In these pages, you will discover advice that will help you throughout your stay. This book will not tell you exact addresses or store hours but instead will give you excitement and knowledge from a local that you may not find in other smaller print travel books.

Travel like a local. Slow down, stay in one place, and get to know the people and the culture. By the time you finish this book, you will be eager and prepared to travel to your next destination.

>TOURIST

TABLE OF CONTENTS

BOOK DESCRIPTION
TABLE OF CONTENTS
DEDICATION
ABOUT THE AUTHOR
HOW TO USE THIS BOOK
FROM THE PUBLISHER
OUR STORY
WELCOME TO
> TOURIST
INTRODUCTION
1. How to Get to Poznań
2. Huge Saving with Special Offers
3. Download These Apps Before Arriving
4. Learn Some Phrases in Polish
5. Have Knowledge About History of Poznań
6. Currency to Carry
7. Best Times to Visit
8. Remember to Bring These Items with You
9. Bear in Mind These Rules
10. Getting Around Poznań
11. Bike? You Have Come to the Right Place!
12. Be Ready to Travel Through Time
13. See the Billy Goats at Noon

14. One of The Most Impressive Baroque Sacral Edifices in Poland
15. Go Out of the Touristic Places
16. The Heart of Poznań
17. Plan to Visit Lake Malta
18. The Other Places to See
19. Watch a Soccer Match in INEA Stadium
20. Take a Stroll Through the Citadel Park
21. Have You Ever Heard Croissant Museum?
22. Meet with New Animals
23. Smell the Charming Fragrance of Thousands of Plants
24. KontenerART
25. Stay Safe
26. Free Walking Tours
27. A Café Which Will Warm the Cockles of Your Heart
28. Choices for Stopping Sweet Cravings
29. Suggestion for Coffeeholic People
30. What is this queue?
31. Explore Street Foods
32. Tastes Some Alcoholic Drinks
33. The Best Pancakes in Poznań
34. The Kingdom of Potato
35. The Way to People's Heart is Through Pierogi
36. Shopping Time

37. Shopping Mall or Old Brewery? Or Both of them?
38. The Smiling Red Ladybug
39. Souvenirs to Bring Home
40. The Amazing Campaign Called Half Price
41. Where to Stay
42. Do you need to relax?
43. Have a good time with you children together
44. The Center of Culture, Poznań
45. Take a Look at the Events on Facebook
46. Festivals
47. Get Wet on "Wet Monday"
48. Night Life in Poznań
49. Stroll Through the Streets of Poznań in Nightfall
50. What Is This Place Going to Teach You?

TOP REASONS TO BOOK THIS TRIP

50 THINGS TO KNOW ABOUT PACKING LIGHT FOR TRAVEL

Packing and Planning Tips

Travel Questions

Travel Bucket List

NOTES

DEDICATION

This book is dedicated to my family who has provided me with all kinds of opportunities until this age. I am grateful to notably my mother and father because If they had not put their support behind me, maybe I could not have made something of myself. Also, I owe my thanks to my girlfriend Özge who always stand by me and come through for me at least as much as my family.

ABOUT THE AUTHOR

Serkan is a writer, traveler, photographer, and English-Turkish translator. His biggest dream was to be a traveler with his backpack on his back. He has chased this dream over the years. He learned English and got into a university. He became entitled to study English Language and Literature. He has traveled around 33 cities in Turkey by hitchhiking. He did not content himself with this and he went to study in Poland for 6 months. He has traveled 9 countries and 20 cities in Europe with a little money. He has an ebullient spirit. He loves to discover new places by traveling and immortalize the moment by taking photos where he goes.

>TOURIST

HOW TO USE THIS BOOK

The Greater Than a Tourist book series was written by someone who has lived in an area for over three months. The goal of this book is to help travelers either dream or experience different locations by providing opinions from a local. The author has made suggestions based on their own experiences. Please do your own research before traveling to the area in case the suggested places are unavailable.

Travel Advisories: As a first step in planning any trip abroad, check the Travel Advisories for your intended destination.
https://travel.state.gov/content/travel/en/traveladvisories/traveladvisories.html

FROM THE PUBLISHER

Traveling can be one of the most important parts of a person's life. The anticipation and memories that you have are some of the best. As a publisher of the Greater Than a Tourist book series, as well as the popular 50 Things to Know book series, we strive to help you learn about new places, spark your imagination, and inspire you. Wherever you are and whatever you do I wish you safe, fun, and inspiring travel.

Lisa Rusczyk Ed. D.
CZYK Publishing

OUR STORY

Traveling is a passion of the "Greater than a Tourist" series creator. Lisa studied abroad in college, and for their honeymoon Lisa and her husband toured Europe. During her travels to Malta, an older man tried to give her some advice based on his own experience living on the island since he was a young boy. She was not sure if she should talk to the stranger but was interested in his advice. When traveling to some places she was wary to talk to locals because she was afraid that they weren't being genuine. Through her travels, Lisa learned how much locals had to share with tourists. Lisa created the "Greater Than a Tourist" book series to help connect people with locals. A topic that locals are very passionate about sharing.

>TOURIST

WELCOME TO
> TOURIST

INTRODUCTION

*"Man cannot discover new
oceans unless he has the courage to
lose sight of the shore."*

– Andre Gide

I lived in Poznań for about 6 months thanks to the Erasmus Student Exchange Programme which offers university students a possibility of studying or doing an internship abroad in another country. I was fascinated by Poznań for the duration of my stay. Likewise, I am also going to try to make you feel the mystical and peaceful atmosphere of Poznań that is a witness to history with famous and historical houses and buildings. The historic buildings are so well preserved that you can feel like you traveled through time while you are walking through the streets of Poznań. So, would you like to travel through time? If yes, what are you still waiting for?

>TOURIST

1. HOW TO GET TO POZNAŃ

The first option is to go to Poznań in your own car. The city has excellent connections from the west into Germany via the E30 and E65. The E30 continues east to Warsaw and road conditions are generally good.

The other one is by plane. Sometimes you can have difficulty in finding direct flight since Poznań has a small airport and is not one of the most popular destinations in Europe. Nevertheless, there are direct flights to Poznań although not so many. On the other hand, there are also different choices to get to Poznań.

One of the most known and preferred options is Berlin. Firstly, you need to fly to Berlin-Schönefeld Airport (SXF) – the reason why I tell you this airport is that most of the low-cost airlines fly to here – and get on the bus which departs from Schönefeld Airport and goes to Poznań. The distance between Berlin and Poznań is 250 km and it takes almost 3.30 hours to arrive.

The Other one is to fly to Warsaw directly. Warsaw has 2 airports which are called Chopin and Modlin. Modlin is an airport where the low-cost airlines always prefer. So, you can find cheaper flight tickets to Modlin Airport. However, it makes sense to fly to Chopin Airport since it is close to the city center if you can find a cheap ticket. Let's get back to Modlin Airport. I am sorry to say that the city center is a bit far from Modlin Airport. It is actually located almost 40 km from Warsaw. You need to go to the city center and get on the bus in order to arrive Poznań. You have 3 options which consist of train, bus, and taxi to arrive city center. It is important to know that the trains do not depart directly from the airport but from Modlin train station. It takes between 4,5 and 5 hours to arrive Poznań.

The last one is to fly to Prague and go to Poznań by getting on the bus. I do not recommend you because this is the most tiring option among the others. You had better not to prefer this option unless you are really in trouble. Because it is both too far and a bit more expensive. When I went to Prague from Poznań by bus, it took almost 7.30 hours. It was completely torturing.

In my humble opinion, fly to Schönefeld Airport, grab some coffee, get on the bus and enjoy the journey by sipping the coffee together with the increasing excitement and happiness every minute as long as coming close to Poznań.

>TOURIST

2. HUGE SAVING WITH SPECIAL OFFERS

The fact that sometimes there are not many flights to an airport means that you can find cheap tickets with amazing special offers. Poznań- Ławica Airport is one of these airports. I have traveled to many countries in Europe by buses and planes by taking these opportunities like special offers so far. Even sometimes, there are such amazing special offers that you can find a ticket for the prices like 1 Euro which you probably cannot believe your eyes when you see it. If you want to find the tickets like these, you should be flexible. Because the special offers are abruptly showed up in general and so you need to check it out all the time. However, I can assure you that you cannot give up giving chase to cheap tickets after you take pleasure in finding a cheap ticket for once.

Here is a bunch of companies that have the special offers for you and offer you cheap tickets;

*Ryanair: This is the most known and preferred low-cost airline. It operates from 84 bases connecting 35 countries across Europe and North Africa. It usually prefers to fly to smaller airports. I flew to Berlin (SXF) from Brussels (BRU) for 15 Euro.

*Wizzair: It has its largest hub at Budapest Airport with over 60 destinations. Although not as much as Ryanair, it also serves many countries across Europe. I flew to Dortmund (DTM) from Poznań (POZ) for 9 Euro. Also, I flew to Berlin (SXF) from Budapest (BUD) for 19 Euro.

*Flixbus: This is the most known and preferred coach company. It offers intercity bus service in Europe and the United States. The network includes approximately 120,000 daily connections to 1,700+ destinations in 28 countries. You can arrive Poznań by this bus that departs from Berlin Schönefeld Airport. I have traveled to so many countries by these buses with low prices. I went to Poznań from Warsaw for the low price like 0.99 złoty.

3. DOWNLOAD THESE APPS BEFORE ARRIVING

When I first arrived Poznań from Turkey, I could not likely have found where it was or which bus or tram I needed to take in order to arrive there if Marta (my mentor) had not picked me up from the bus station and carry me my dormitory. Moreover, we just were looking at each other when someone asked me

\>TOURIST

something because I did not understand what he/she was saying. The funny thing is that I was responding to him/her in Turkish while he/she was saying something in Polish as if we understood each other. If you do not want to be on the hook like me, you had better download the apps which I tell you.

*Jakdojade: This is definitely one of the first apps that you need to download before arriving Poznań. All the things which you wonder or want to learn are in this app: Which bus or tram do I need to take in order to arrive where I want to go? How can I learn the current timetables? And so on… Furthermore, you can buy tickets in the app. It also reminds you when to set off and get off. This app will be your fellow traveler on your journey!

*Pyszne: Are you hungry? This app is the largest website and app in Poland where you can order food online. The whole restaurants from Poznań in one easily available in one place. You can also pay online via various payments options. If you are tired and stay in Airbnb, You can order food with fast and the meal will be on the way to you in no time.

*Google Maps: This is a map app which you can use online or offline. Before arriving Poznań, you download the map of Poznań. Although you do not have Wi-Fi or internet, you can benefit from it.

*Nextbike: This is an app which is my most favorite app and commonly used in Poznań. It shows you all available bikes and stations in real time. You can ride a bike with your account in the app which you have activated before.

*English-polish & Polish-English offline dictionary: It is a free offline dictionary (vocabulary) with easy and functional user interface, covers over 110.000 words. It saves your life since it is offline dictionary. You can also download Google Translation apart from this. However, it requires internet or Wi-Fi.

4. LEARN SOME PHRASES IN POLISH

Polish is considered one of the hardest languages in the world to learn. If you ask me what I learn in Polish, I learned only basic words although I lived in Poznań for 6 months. I have learned most of them consciously or unconsciously. For instance, I learned how to say 'excuse me' when I hindered someone from passing and he/she asked me permission for passing in markets or I associated the rice with the word written on the package when I went to the

>TOURIST

supermarket to buy some rice. I have put together the basic phrases that will help you on your journey.

*Dzień dobry' (jine-dobree)

Meaning: Good day

Saying hello is one of the most important things which you can make sincere contact with local people. It literally means 'good morning' but you can use both in the morning and late at night. You can always hear this word in markets.

*'Proszę' (proshe)

Meaning: Please

When you go to grab something to drink or something to eat, you can say this word.

*'Dziękuję' (jen-koo-yea)

Meaning: Thank you

This is the other necessary phrase in Poland. You can use after you have received your beer or coffee or something like that.

*'Przepraszam' (psh-she-pra-sham)

Meaning: Sorry, Excuse me

This was the second phrase when I arrived Poznań. Also, I do not know why but I like to say this phrase.

*'Nie rozumiem' (nie ro-zoo-me-em)

Meaning: I don't understand

This is really lifesaving phrase. You can say this phrase to him/her if someone come to you and say something.

5. HAVE KNOWLEDGE ABOUT HISTORY OF POZNAŃ

I believe that the most important thing needed to be done before traveling is to get information about the history of the city and country that you are going to visit in order to feel the spirit of that city better. I feel incompetent unless I get information about its history before going to a city. I think that the most beautiful feeling on the journey is to be able to feel same emotion as the people in the past. You are situated in the same place where the people in the past walked around once upon a time.

The city was founded as a 9th-century settlement on the easily defensible island of Ostrów Tumski, during the reign of Poland's first ruler, Duke Mieszko I. Mieszko's son, the first Polish king, Bolesław Chrobry, further strengthened the island, and the troops of the Holy Roman Empire that conquered the region in 1005 didn't even bother to lay siege to it. The Bohemian Prince Bratislav (Brzetysław), however, liked a challenge and damaged the town considerably in 1038. This marked the end for Poznań as the royal seat (though kings were buried here until 1296), as subsequent rulers chose Kraków as their home. From the mid-17th century on, Swedish, Prussian and Russian invasions, together with a series of natural disasters, battered the city. In the Second Partition of 1793, Poznań fell under Prussian occupation and was renamed Posen, later becoming part of Germany and experiencing steady industrial growth up to the outbreak of WWI. The city fell into German hands once more during WWII, and was incorporated into Hitler's Third Reich. In 1945, the battle for its liberation took a month and did a huge amount of damage. In the postwar era, Poznań was one of the first cities to feel the forceful hand of the communist regime, during a massive worker strike in June 1956. The spontaneous demonstration, cruelly crushed by tanks, turned out to be the first of a wave of popular protests on the long and painful road to overcoming communist rule.

6. CURRENCY TO CARRY

Poland has its own currency called Zloty (PLN). Unfortunately, you cannot pay to pay with Euro or US Dollars in most places. That's why you need to exchange your money before arriving or after arriving in the city or you can pay with your credit cards in most places. Your bank will automatically exchange your money from Zloty to Euro or US Dollars (this method was one of the methods which I commonly used). I suggest banks you to exchange your money. Banks are the easiest places you can find, to get Poland's money. You can also withdraw cash from ATMs. Pick ATMs located inside a bank or a busy shopping center. These are considered to be the most secure ATMs. I always used to withdraw cash from BZ WBK. Moreover, it has an English option. The other most known banks are Bank Pekao Sa, ING Bank, PKO Bank Polski. The other choice is to find smaller exchange bureaus called 'Kantor'. However, bear in mind that they usually buy dearer and sell cheaper than banks. If you are in trouble in the matter of finding banks or ATMs or Kantors, do not feel panic and just ask nice local people. They will show you the way.

>TOURIST

7. BEST TIMES TO VISIT

The best time to visit is spring and summer months. Because, there are always a lot of events such as open-air cinemas or theatres, open-air concerts, block parties, dance shows, music and food festivals and so on. On average, the warmest months are July and August and the most crowded months are also July and August. Besides, Warta River, Old Market Square, Park Cytadela is showier in summer. The spring and summer seasons are also the perfect time to explore on foot or rent a bike.

I do not recommend you to travel Poznań in winter months. Because the weather is far too cold in Poznań to be enjoyable for warm weather travelers. In Poznań, January is the coldest month of the year. But if you like winter and want to be chilled to the bone, I can give you some advice about what to do in winter months in Poznań. Especially on Christmas eve, the colorful booths pleasing to the eye are built in Freedom Square (Plac Wolnosci). You can get warm even if you just watch the dance of colorful lights. Besides, there is a fair called Poznań Beer Fair which crowds of people attend every year. During the Beer Fair, not only you can taste in dozens of beers but also you can talk with professional brewers, bloggers and all those who just love good beer and you can exchange experiences, or learn something new. You can also visit any museums in Poznań at your sweet will.

Here are museums;
National Museum in Poznań
Museum of the History of Poznań
Painting and Sculpture Gallery
Musical Instruments Museum
Applied Arts Museum
Archaeological Museum
The Museum of Poznań Uprising 1956
Literary Museum of Henryk Sienkiewicz
Archbishopric Museum
Motoring Museum

8. REMEMBER TO BRING THESE ITEMS WITH YOU

If you plan to visit Poznań in winter, you have to dress warmly. Do not forget your scarf, gloves, beanie, thermal underwear, waterproof boot and so on. Also, you can bring your hand cream to prevent cracked skin due to cold.

> TOURIST

If you plan to visit in autumn or spring, you need to bring a raincoat, umbrella and waterproof boot with you. Because the weather in Poznań is rainy in autumn and spring in general.

Finally, abundantly memory to save your photos and videos!

9. BEAR IN MIND THESE RULES

There is no doubt that Polish people are one of the best societies to follow the rules properly. Even, they are so disciplined that they are probably not Polish if you see the people who break the rules. I admire them on this matter. To be frank, I have broken a lot of rules unconsciously in the beginning. This put me to shame. I got used to following the rules sometime later and then I realized how necessary some rules were. Here are the most important ones among them;

*Smoking & drinking in public places

It is not legal to smoke in most of the public spaces. Be careful especially at the train station and bus stops. Some pubs and clubs let its customer smoke by creating special areas where smoking is allowed.

Drinking alcohol in public spaces is also considered illegal. Apart from the places such as pubs and clubs, it is strictly forbidden to drink alcohol in the streets, parks, buses, trams and so on. A minor detail: If you come to Poznań in Summer, grab a beer and go to directly Warta River. It is not forbidden to drink alcohol around the Warta River.

*Stamp your bus/tram ticket

In Poland, it is not enough to just buy a ticket and get on a bus or tram. In addition to this, you need to validate your ticket by inserting your ticket into the machines found on the bus or tram too. The machine will stamp it with the date, time and your route. If the officer comes to check out the tickets, he takes a look at this information. Please make sure that your ticket is out of date.

*Jaywalking and road safety

This rule is quite important. Wandering across the street anywhere you like is illegal even if there is no traffic in sight. You have to use the crosswalk to cross the road. What do you need to do in the crosswalk without lights? According to Polish laws, Cars have to stop if there is somebody already on a crossing or somebody who attempts to cross. Also, you have to wait at red lights for pedestrians even if there is no car.

>TOURIST

10. GETTING AROUND POZNAŃ

Buses and trams are quite efficient, cheap and fast. But I think the most efficient and the best way is on foot. Because, the city is already small. However, being small does not mean that it is not beautiful. You will already see how beautiful Poznań is while taking a walk.

Poznań is crisscrossed by 19 tram routes (of which one runs at night), and 118 bus lines (20 at night). Buses and trams run every 12-20 minutes from 4:30am to 11:00pm (day service) and every half an hour from 11 pm. to 4.30am (night service). Timetables are available at the website of the City Transport Company or Jakdojade application. Single tickets are available: for 10 mins and for 40 mins as well as for 24-, 48- and 72 hours. The best option for a longer ride through the city or a few days long stay in Poznań is a 24-hours or a 3-days ticket. You can buy transport tickets from automated machines found on most buses and trams or on Jakdojade application. If you buy a ticket from automated machines, please do not forget to validate your ticket by inserting them into machines. Also, most taxis are reliable and use their meters without any fiddling around. But still be careful.

11. BIKE? YOU HAVE COME TO THE RIGHT PLACE!

Poznań is one of the cities where I take great pleasure in riding a bike. Because there are well-developed bike paths and drivers attach importance to the rider as well. Even sometimes some bike paths move through the main road. It means that sometimes you push ahead with cars on the same road. Even, you have to stop at red lights with cars. They never block the bike paths. This makes you feel special. Because they show to respect you. Furthermore, renting a bike is as easy as apple pie. The most popular way of renting a bike is the Next Bike system like I mentioned before. A prior online registration is obligatory before renting. I recommend you to download the app before arriving. You can easily find a lot of terminals to rent a bike. After renting, you can go wherever you want. The bike paths which you can get in touch with nature like Park Cytadela are among the most popular routes. One of the most attractive city biking paths leads around the Malta Lake as well. And one of my favorite bike paths is found around Warta River. Ride a bike around Warta at sunset in particular. It is really worth to see. It is incredible pleasure

>TOURIST

Tip: The first 20 minutes of bike usage is free of charge. When you rent a bike, you do not need to come back to the terminal that you rent to deliver the bike. You can place the bike in any terminal that you first see. If you arrive any terminal before 20 minutes, place it in that terminal and rent another one. If you do it every 20 minutes, you will ride a bike and stroll around without paying a red cent.

Have a nice ride!

12. BE READY TO TRAVEL THROUGH TIME

I was going taking an uttermost pleasure in inching along on the cobblestones of the city. While the wind of tranquility was blowing in the city, each part of my body was covered by a quietness as well. Although the buildings were uttermost old and tumbledown, this did not rag on me, on the contrary, it let me get into the feelings which I could not depict. I have had a small but sharp pain which I felt in the midst of my rib cage. Maybe I was feeling the same pain as the pain of the children who scampered around the place where I was standing now and then passed away in wartime. I was going back in time in every step. My all perceptions were getting changed. I was probably not where I had been but I was where I wanted to be. I could have thought wrong. I could have misunderstood. But I could not have felt wrong. I was able to feel that I went back in time. The whole sounds died away. I did not know what time it was. When I consulted my watch, I realized that my watch stopped working. I lost track of time. As if the time stopped. I could not even hear my voice in this ear-splitting silence. When I came to Old Market Square, I could hear the sound of the horse-drawn carriages. There was a pretty bustle around. The old black and white lives which we always saw on the old pictures were not actually that much black and white. Even, their lives were more colorful than ours. I saw the employees who tried to restore the buildings damaged in wartime, the children who did not take their mother's advice and were bustling around, the guardant teenage girls who hoped to see the boys who they fell in love behind the windows and the soldiers who devoted themselves to be loyal to the homeland, Republic of Poland. Everything was in harmony. The more I walked, the more I was going back in time, going back the oldest time. I suddenly tripped and fell into the ground. That really hurt. However, the only thing that made my heart bleed was to turn back at the moment instead of being hurt. I really turned back at the moment. I saw a large crowd of faces when I raised my head. When I consulted my watch again, I saw that my watch was working this time. I explored the notion of time again.

I do not know whether I will begin time travel once again or not but all I know was that this city and Old Market Square has a magical atmosphere.

13. SEE THE BILLY GOATS AT NOON

The first time I went to Old Market Square, I saw a large crowd of faces. I did not have any idea what they were doing or what they were looking at. They were looking at a clock with mechanical billy goats found in Renaissance Town Hall. Every day, as the clock strikes noon, on the tower above the clock a door opens, and two billy goats appear. By the way, I want to remind you that billy goat is the symbol of Poznań. Then, they butt their horned heads 12 times. If you cannot arrive Old Town Square (Stary Rynek or Old Market Square) before 12 pm, there is a vintage billy goat mechanism on display inside the Town Hall. Also, I recommend you to take a look at the images of the great and the good people on the Town Hall.

Tip: If you want to view the city panorama, go to the top of the Collegium Altum of the Economic University of Poznan which is big orange building. Moreover, it is free.

Address: Stary Rynek 1, 61-768 Poznań, Poland

14. ONE OF THE MOST IMPRESSIVE BAROQUE SACRAL EDIFICES IN POLAND

Did you get enough the pleasure of history? Of course, no. After a long time travel, let's go on without breaking the spell. You can see Fara Church's white-pink building from any place in the Old Market Square. The collegiate church of the parish church district under the invocation of Our Lady of Perpetual Succour and St Mary Magdalene is one of the most exquisite examples of Baroque architecture in Poland. When you wander in the church, the mystical and numinous atmosphere of the church will jar every bone in your body for sure. Also, in summer, you have a chance to listen to all the famous organs of the master craftsman Ladegast daily during the free concerts (from September to June only on Saturdays). Apart from these months, you can listen to them in every Sunday.

Address: Klasztorna 11, 61-779 Poznań, Poland

15. GO OUT OF THE TOURISTIC PLACES

One of the things which people are afraid in this world is to get lost as well. Because going beyond the ordinary or limits gives them a scare. Do not read the same page continually. Head over unknown. Get lost and do not know where you are going. Your desire to explore new places always takes precedence over the risk of being lost or in trouble. For example, feel the raindrops falling from the sky on the back of your neck while you are wandering around the unknown streets of Poznań. Take shelter in the first place that you will see. Who knows maybe you will catch a smell which makes you feel like a child who chases rainbows. Maybe you will feel some emotions you have never experienced. Maybe you will thank the rain which causes you to come to that place that you experience the emotions you have never experienced before. And you will notice that you get to the point where you realize traveling is truly bliss.

Each street of Poznań is special. Do not hesitate to explore them.

16. THE HEART OF POZNAŃ

According to some people, the heart of Poznań is Old Market Square or Freedom Square. However, according to me, the heart of Poznań is the Warta River. Warta is the main river that runs through Poznan. I spent most of my 6 months in there. Well, what makes it so special for me? I am in love with the sea. I cannot even think a life without the sea. When I arrived Poznań, this was one of my biggest problems. I started to try to find a solution. I explored Malta and Warta. Warta was piqued my curiosity more. I came here and could relax to some extent. In summer and spring, you can see a whole bunch of events and festival over there. The world and his wife come together in Warta to play some games, talk to each other, drink alcohol, grill some sausages, ride bike, skate and so on. I used to grab a beer and go to Warta at sunset in order to hang out with my friends and grill some sausages.

>TOURIST

Tip: I have encountered a game in here which was played by young and I had never seen before. That's why I liked so much and was very intrigued. Even, there is an event about this game. I do not know the rules of the game in the strict sense but I will try to tell you to the best of my recollection. Firstly, People who want to play this game come together with their unopened beers and a ball and then people are divided into two groups according to the number of people. Apart from these people, a referee is determined as well. These two teams are supposed to be face to face. Everyone opens their own beers and put it in front of them. An empty beer bottle is also put down between them. The teams throw the ball in order to knock it over by in regular turn. If one team misses off the target, the turn switches to the other team. If one team hits the target (the empty beer bottle), People in the team who hits the target can drink their beers until someone in the other team brings the beer bottle upright position and comes back. When he/she comes back, they cannot drink beer any longer. The first team which runs out of their beer over wins. If you see some people who play this game, you can ask them whether you can join them or not.

17. PLAN TO VISIT LAKE MALTA

Lake Malta is an artificial lake in Poznań. It is better than Warta but it is farther than Warta. You can create a bike route which Lake Malta is included. For most people, it is a place of relaxing weekend walks and active leisure, it is also a great place to relax and drink a beer with your friends. If you want to complete one lap of the lake, it would probably take about an hour or so on foot. In summer and spring, there are family-friendly attractions and activities which consist of miniature golf, sunbathe, cycling, a spa complex, water park and sports, pools, open-air performances, rowing and so on.

Lake Malta is situated just to the east of the city center. I will tell you how you arrive there apart from taxi and bike;

*From the main train station: Take tram number 6 from the 'Poznań Główny' stop (walk just past the Avenida shopping center going east) directly to 'Baraniaka'. The journey takes about 14 minutes.

*From the Old Town Square: Take tram number 3, 16, or 17 from either 'Pl. Wielkopolski' or 'Małe Garbary' to 'Rondo Śródka'.

\>TOURIST

18. THE OTHER PLACES TO SEE

While you are wandering around Poznań, you keep being dazzled by beautiful places, historical buildings of Poznań. Let's take a look at the other places to visit;

*Ostrów Tumski

It is a quiet island, with a permanent population consisting mostly of bishops, priests and monks. It is known as Cathedral Island. Even, there is an interesting story of this island. According to the prolific legend, three Slav brothers known as Lech, Czech and Rus met on this tiny island after not seeing each other for many years. To commemorate their reunion the brothers named the place 'Poznać,' after the Polish word for 'to meet'. I even recommend you to visit only magnificent Poznań Cathedral itself.

* Śródka

After you wander around Ostrów Tumski, the next step will be Śródka. If you are not sated with history, explore Śródka which there are ancient ducal settlements and exposes you to travel through time again with packed full of points which brims over with history. I especially recommend you to see 'A

Śródka Tale' Mural which there is a famous mural made with 3D creation.

*Jordan Bridge

It a red bridge which functions as a bridge between Ostrów Tumski and Śródka.

Address: most Biskupa Jordana, 61-124 Poznań, Poland

*Great Theatre

The name is a bit of a misnomer as the Great Theatre today is home to opera and ballet. Built in 1910 by Max Littman as a city theatre house for the German population of what was then Prussian 'Posen,' the last German performance was held in 1919 before the Wielkopolska Uprising. Plays continued to be performed until 1924 when it became the full-time home to the Polish Opera. Under the Nazis the building received a renovation led by the German architect Paul Bankarten but was soon caught up in the whirlwind of WWII where it served as a hospital for wounded German soldiers between 1943 and 1945.

Address: Fredry 9, 61-701 Poznań, Poland

* Royal Castle

You can easily arrive there on foot from Old Market Square. Once the pride of Poznań, the original construction was begun approximately 1249 by

Przemysł I - Duke of the Piast dynasty who had chosen Poz as his capital. Its fortunes took a serious turn for the worse in early 18th century when it was sacked several times in quick succession by the Swedes, the Russians, and then disgruntled nobles. In 1959 the decision was taken to rebuild Raczyński's contribution to the hill, which today houses the Applied Arts Museum. Between 2010 and 2016 the castle underwent a total restoration, and is now fully open, including the castle tower, observation decks, and Prince Przemysł I Hall.

Address: Góra Przemysła 1, 60-101 Poznań, Poland

19. WATCH A SOCCER MATCH IN INEA STADIUM

One day I heard shouting noises while I was just wandering around the streets of Poznań. I did not know where the noise was coming from but these shouting noises brought with earth-shaking footsteps. It was such a strong noise that I could see that the leaves in the ground were vibrating because of the noises. I felt that the noise was coming closer to me. I saw that passionate and crazy soccer fans were coming to me with football torches in their hand. I did not need to comprehend what they were saying because I could feel the same emotions as them. They were heading over the INEA Stadium like two lovers who are head over heels in love with each other by keeping the flame alive in their hearts. I felt so sad that I could not join them. INEA Stadium turns into a hell due to the red football torches in general.

If you want to be part of them and a witness to this visual feast, just a match ticket and go to INEA Stadium.

Address: Bułgarska 17, 60-320 Poznań, Poland

20. TAKE A STROLL THROUGH THE CITADEL PARK

Park Cytadela in Poznań is a large park on the site of Fort Winiary, a 19th-century fortified area north of the city center. It contains a military museum, military cemeteries, and the remains of some of the fortifications. The park is so big that sometimes you can think that there are no people in the park. Just even watching happy children who scamper around can make you happy. When you visit the military museum, you can think of all the pain Poland as a nation had gone through. Also, especially the headless sculptures can compel you to think. Because it is so important what artist who made them wants to tell us. You will need to give them your consideration.

Put aside your problems and sorrow and just wandering around with bird calls and sounds of nature. Throw yourself at mother nature.

Note: The museum is closed on Monday's.

21. HAVE YOU EVER HEARD CROISSANT MUSEUM?

The Croissant Museum in Poznan is a place where you will learn about the history of the city and about the Croissant legend. Croissants are baked specifically for St. Martin's Day (November 11th). It is a very enjoyable and educational museum. They tell you the history of the croissant and teach about the process of making local croissants in one room. The presenters are very humoristic and vigorous and speak both Polish and English languages. It is like a stand-up show more than a museum. Besides tasting the amazing taste, you will have the chance to participate in the cooking also. The presentation takes around 50 minutes, booking not necessary, but recommended; check their website for the running times.

I strongly recommend you all travelers to visit this museum!

Address: wejście od, Klasztorna 23, 61-779 Poznań, Poland

22. MEET WITH NEW ANIMALS

There are 2 zoos that you can visit in Poznań. The smallest one is Old (Stare) Zoo. The other one which is bigger is New (Nowe) Zoo.

*New (Nowe) Zoo

To the east of Lake Malta is the New Zoo which can be reached on foot or by the small steam train service. The zoo is comprised of pine and mixed forests, which serve as a natural habitat for around 140 different species and more than 2000 animals. You can use trains found in the zoo to make their tour of the Zoo or you can visit the Zoo on foot.

Address: Krańcowa 81, 61-048 Poznań, Poland

*Old (Stare) Zoo

>TOURIST

I do not recommend you to visit this Zoo since it is both more uncared and smaller than New Zoo. Do not lose your time by visiting this Zoo.

Address: Zwierzyniecka 19, 60-814 Poznań, Poland

23. SMELL THE CHARMING FRAGRANCE OF THOUSANDS OF PLANTS

Do you want to get lost within the charming fragrance of thousands of plants? Not only Poznan appeals to your eyes with its historical buildings or your stomach with its delicious foods but also it appeals to your nose with its charming fragrances. Be ready to   be delighted by the Poznań Botanical Garden.

The Poznań Botanical Garden has been established between 1922 and 1925. In an area of 22 hectares, it has a collection of over 7 thousand species and varieties of plants from nearly all of the Earth's climate and plant classifications. Poznań's lovely Botanical Garden boasts a vast 22 hectares and over 7,000 varieties of plants from almost every kind of climate and ecosystem in the world. The park includes several greenhouses, a snazzy two-storey exhibition pavilion with a gallery, shop, and cafe, several enormous standing stones they took great trouble to bring here, and a lovely ballerina fountain designed by Margaret Węcławska - a graduate of the Poz Academy of Fine Arts.

Address: Dąbrowskiego 165, 60-594 Poznań, Poland

24. KONTENERART

An interesting art space set in a courtyard constructed from shipping containers, on the banks of the Warta. It is surrounded by an artificial beach. The atmosphere is great, you can feel the good vibes, and meet there with friends or just go on your own to relax and inspire yourself. In summer and spring, there are concerts, dance lessons and so on.

Tip: Climb the stairs for a second-story seat that offers a view of the river and the ideal perch for people-watching.

>TOURIST

25. STAY SAFE

Poland is a quite safe and wonderful country. I have also never encountered any problem, any racism in Poznań for the duration of my stay. Even if you stroll around the city in the dead of night, nobody would harm a hair on your head. But still, I do not recommend you to stroll around Park Cytadela at midnight. Sometimes, drunkard can tangle with each other around the clubs. You had better steer away from them at that moment.

26. FREE WALKING TOURS

I have occurred at the same time as free walking tour by mistake while wandering around Old Market Square. I have joined them and I really liked the tour. If you do not have enough time to think about where you need to go or see, this tour which is also in so many countries apart from Poznań provide you with the opportunity of seeing the most important places in Poznań in about 1 hour 45 minutes. Also, if you want to get more information about history of Poznań or famous buildings, it will be really beneficial to you. All you need to do is to go to Old Market Square (Stary Rynek), in front of the Old Town Hall and look for the guide with yellow umbrella. Bear in mind that the guide waits up until almost 7 people join in the tour. They do not accept groups of over 7 people on our regular tours on principle. Finally, the people who want to donate (it is not compulsory) can give money to the guide when the tour is over. Here is its times and dates;

    Oct-Nov: Thursday, Friday, Saturday & Sunday at 11:45 AM

    Dec-Apr: Saturday & Sunday at 11:45 AM

    May-Jun: Thursday, Friday, Saturday & Sunday at 11:45 AM

    Jul-Sep: everyday 11:45 AM

27. A CAFÉ WHICH WILL WARM THE COCKLES OF YOUR HEART

If you go to Poznań in winter, you are probably chilled to the marrow after a while although you still bundle yourself up against the bitter cold. I will carry you a café which offers the best hot chocolate of Poznań. The name of this café is 'Cacao Republika' located between Royal Castle (Zamek Królewski) and Old Market Square. It has an authentic and modest concept. There is all the kind of chocolates. The smell

>TOURIST

of the hot chocolate can make you feel mentally alert. When you take a swig, it will warm the cockles of your heart for sure and tug at your heartstrings. You can drink your hot chocolate sip by sip while you are watching the snowflakes. When you get through it, you will be deeply in sorrow.

I can assure you that you cannot forget its taste!
Address: Zamkowa 7, 61-768 Poznań, Poland

28. CHOICES FOR STOPPING SWEET CRAVINGS

There is no doubt that the first thing coming to mind is Rogal Świętomarciński (St Martin's Croissant) when it comes to Poznań. It is one of the most recognizable and undoubtedly tastiest symbols of Poznań. During the upcoming Independence Day celebrations on November 11th, combined with the names-day of Święty Marcin Street (St. Martin's), nearly a million of the crescent-shaped, poppy-seed filled pastries will be eaten. Also, there is a dessert shop called Stara Pączkarnia. You can taste famous, delicious and cheap local deserts and the best donuts in there. You should visit this shop! The address of

Bakery - Confectionery Liczbańscy: 23 Lutego 61-743, 61-741 Poznań, Poland

The address of Stara Pączkarnia: Dąbrowskiego 26, 60-841 Poznań, Poland

29. SUGGESTION FOR COFFEEHOLIC PEOPLE

If you are coffeeholic and need to drink coffee immediately, pin back your ears.

You can buy a takeaway coffee from Costa Coffee found in Old Market Square and stroll around the city with your coffee. Or I can recommend you to buy a delicious and cheap takeaway coffee from a hawker in front of the monument of Freedom Square.

If you want to drink your coffee while sitting and resting, go to remained hidden Organic Coffee. All the coffee in Organic Coffee is quite good, delicious and cheap. Finally, one of the best coffee shops is Cezve Kawiarnia. You can taste Turkish coffee if you have never tasted in your life. Not only there is coffee, but also there are various kinds of delicious foods. I highly recommend you to taste!

The address of Costa Coffee: Stary Rynek 53/54, 61-771 Poznań, Poland

>TOURIST

The address of Cezve Kawiarnia: 73, Święty Marcin, 61-717 Poznań, Poland

The address of Organic Coffee: 1, Rondo Kaponiera, 60-829 Poznań, Poland

30. WHAT IS THIS QUEUE?

While I was going to Freedom Square, I saw scores of people who were waiting for something in front of a shop. I had never seen such a long queue like this up to that time in Poznań. I wondered what this queue was. I saw that it was an ice cream shop called Kolorowa. I thought that the fact that there was that much a long queue in front of one shop meant that this shop was very famous and good. I also came into the line without further loss of time. I have waited for ages. When it was my turn, I had difficulty in communicating with the ice cream seller since she did not know English very well. Somehow, we have agreed. After I tasted it once, I said to myself that it was definitely worth the wait. The snickers one and lemon one were really good.

If you like ice cream, you have to make a visit here!

Address: 27 Grudnia 21, 61-712 Poznań, Poland

31. EXPLORE STREET FOODS

Sometimes you should not shy away from eating street foods. Because hawkers and vendors offer both cheaper and more delicious local foods of the city where you travel. However, most people think that street foods are not both healthy and hygienic. It is not a problem as long as you eat it in some famous places. I will tell you the name of 2 famous places where I have gone to eat;

*Teatralka. Mała gastronomia

I recommend you to eat Zapiekanka which is an open-face sandwich made of half of a baguette or other long roll of bread, topped with sautéed white mushrooms, cheese and sometimes other ingredients, and toasted until the cheese melts. It is a popular street food in Poland.
Address: Roosevelta 10, 60-823 Poznań, Poland

* Burger Kebab Box

You can eat a kebab sandwich in Burger Kebab Box. Kebab is actually famous in Turkey. Turkey has introduced the world to kebab. And Polish people like to eat kebab so much. Moreover, there is even a song about a girl who is eating kebab. Address: Dąbrowskiego 8, 60-823 Poznań, Poland

>TOURIST

32. TASTES SOME ALCOHOLIC DRINKS

Vodka and beer are most popular among the other alcohols in Poland. Therefore, I am going to take the two on board.

*Vodka

There are hundreds of brands. Nearly all of them are so cheap. But still, there are between 20 and 25 vodka which is worth drinking among them in spite of causing a headache. One of them is Zubrowka Bison with green grass and the other one is Goldwasser which contain gold particle in itself.

*Beer

Poland is the third largest brewer with 70 brands in Europe. Even some brands have been carrying on their beer production without pausing since the 13th century. The beer prices are quite low. When the people in the dark ages drank the germ-infested water which had been waiting for a long time in a barrel, they would be ill. However, when they drank the beer which had been waiting for a long time in a barrel, they would not be ill since the germs did not live in alcohol. That's why it has been always part of Europe culture.

Tyskie, Zywiec, Lech and Zubr are most popular beer brands among them.

33. THE BEST PANCAKES IN POZNAŃ

I cannot say this is a local food of Poznań but I can recommend people who want to eat except local foods, to this restaurant that offers the best pancakes in Poznań. If you want to be as full as a tick beside being delicious and cheap, I invite you to dinner in 'Manekin'. The pancakes are so huge and tasty. There are a lot of pancakes which range from main meals to sweets. All of them more beautiful than one another. Also, the menu is available in English. Firstly, waiters are very kind and cheerful. They meet you at the door and this makes you happy. The only problem is that the place is so popular. That's why you cannot find a place to sit if you come to here in the evening. And also, you can wait a bit to get your meal due to this reason even if you find a place.

Despite everything, I highly recommend it!
Address: Mickiewicza 24, 61-832 Poznań, Poland
Kwiatowa 3, 60-995 Poznań, Poland

>TOURIST

34. THE KINGDOM OF POTATO

The kingdom of Potato has reigned over for a very long time in Poznań. The people love potato so much. The potato was one of the most consumed vegetables in the past in Poznań. Because it was both low cost and easily cooked. Potato is popular now in Poznań as well.

Have you ever eaten in a restaurant where everything is made with potatoes? I recommend you to go to 'Pyrabar' in order to eat incredible foods made with potatoes. When you first go there, you can think that it is an ordinary restaurant but after eating the meal, I am sure you will be pleasantly surprised. The service is fast, food is tasty and served very hot, fresh from the oven. The price is also good. There are English menus. If you want to taste some local food, make a stop in this lovely place. You will not regret it!

Address: Strzelecka 13, 60-846 Poznań, Poland

35. THE WAY TO PEOPLE'S HEART IS THROUGH PIEROGI

The first thing coming to mind is Pierogi when you say Poland. Pierogi are made of a thinly rolled dough with various fillings such as potato, minced meat, cheese, spinach, mushroom, pork, some fruits and so on. All flavors are all delicious and clearly fresh. The Polish word pierogi is plural. That's why pierogi is always served two or usually more. The best pierogi is fried pierogi. So, if you want to taste fried pierogi, you can say 'smazone (sımajone / fried)' to the waiter while giving an order. My favorites are pierogi with spinach, mushroom and cheddar cheese and pierogi with potato and mushroom. You should definitely request 'kysla smotana(sour cream)' and 'kysle mlieko(beverage)' from the waiter.

I recommend you to 'Chatka Babuni' that offers the best and most delicious pierogi in Poznań.

Address: Wrocławska 18, 61-838 Poznań, Poland

36. SHOPPING TIME

There are many shopping centers in Poznań offering many attraction discounts alongside

>TOURIST

shopping. I will tell you most of them apart from Stary Browar which I will mention following.

*Posnania

Posnania offers the largest selection of brands in Poznań. You will find 260 stores as well as 40 restaurants, cafes, a cinema, a bowling alley, a fitness club with a swimming pool.

Address: Pleszewska 1, 61-139 Poznań, Poland

*Avenida

Avenida is one of Wielkopolska's largest shopping centers. Avenida is home to more than 200 shops and 30 restaurants and cafes. The center is in direct vicinity of the bus and train station. If you arrive Poznan with bus or train, you can spend time in this shopping mall.

Address: Matyi 2, 61-586 Poznań, Poland

*Galeria Malta

Galeria Malta was created in one of Poznań's most picturesque areas - at the shore of Lake Malta. The shopping mall houses 170 salons of Poland's most popular local and foreign brands, service points, restaurants, cafes, a modern cinema and a fitness club.

Address: Maltańska 1, 61-131 Poznań, Poland

*Galeria MM

A shopping mall right in the city center for all your shopping needs, be it clothes, a tall caramel frappuccino, make-up, or the sudden urge to go bowling. It is a five-minute walk away from Old Market Square.

Address: Święty Marcin 24, 61-805 Poznań, Poland

Tip: You all ladies will be delighted with this news. Do you want to buy clothes with discounts up to 70 percent? Factory Outlet situated near the southern border of the city offers you discounts of 30-70% all year round. But the only disadvantage is that it is a bit far.

Address: Dębiecka 1, 62-030 Luboń, Poland

37. SHOPPING MALL OR OLD BREWERY? OR BOTH OF THEM?

This building which was the old brewery was converted a shopping mall afterward. The award-winning Stary Browar complex has been dubbed an art, leisure, and shopping extravaganza, and its success a sign of Poznań's economic renaissance. It is home to around stores and restaurants. It is located in the center of Poznań, Poland at 42 Półwiejska Street.

You can find hundreds of shops. However, this shopping mall is a little expensive.

38. THE SMILING RED LADYBUG

The smiling red ladybug? It sounds strange, isn't it? This is a symbol which you can see almost in everywhere in Poland. Keep it on your mind before strolling around. Well, what does it mean? It is a supermarket which is called 'Biedronka' and a smiling red ladybug is on the logo. It is the largest discount supermarket chain in Poland with about 2,823 stores. You can buy everything which you need on the cheap. However, its bad side is that the product range is not so much wide. Also, you can go to Netto, Lidl, Tesco, Aldı, Carrefour, Zabka, Piotr i Paweł apart from Biedronka.

Tip: I used to buy and eat garlic bread and donut with Oreo from Biedronka. You should definitely taste them. But generally, all garlic bread are sold early in the morning. Also, you can buy a grill and some sausages for a song in order to grill in Warta.

39. SOUVENIRS TO BRING HOME

You can find a lot of souvenirs such as magnets, the sculpture of billy goats, lid opener, lighter, Polish flag and whatever you want in Old Market Square.

If you want to buy souvenirs at a cheaper price, you will find the best deals in tourist information shops.

Address: Stary Rynek 59/60, 61-772 Poznań, Poland

*Souvenirs Poznań (Pamiątki z Poznania)

This a place where you can find a lot of beautiful pieces and whatever you want. I really recommend here!

Adress: Wrocławska 25a, 61-838 Poznań, Poland

40. THE AMAZING CAMPAIGN CALLED HALF PRICE

Who doesn't love a good sale? Each year a different weekend in April or May in chosen when prices of hotels, restaurants, bars, museums and other tourist attractions start melting. Museums, attractions, institutions, hotels and restaurants all over the city

>TOURIST

offer their services with a 50% discount. Half Price nearly 180 attractions in and around Poznań are made available.

I know that you go ape over this news!

41. WHERE TO STAY

If you make it your business to travel with the small budget, I recommend you to stay in the hostels which are really cheap and cozy. It is not so important whether a hotel, hostel, Airbnb which you will stay, close to Old Market Square or not since Poznań is not that big city. I will write the options down here;
*Hostel
Hostel Jeżyce Poznań
Blooms Boutique Hostel Inn and Apartments
By the Way Hostel
Dizzy Daisy Hostel
Hostel Poznan
Melody Hostel

*Hotel
Hotel Ibis
Hotel 222
Hotel Naramowice

Hotel Tango
Hotel Mercure
Hotel Sheraton
Novotel Poznan Malta

*Airbnb

If you are two or more, I absolutely recommend to you stay in Airbnb. It is quite comfortable, cheap and easy. Before arriving Poznań, download the Airbnb application and rent a home.

Tip: I have stayed in Jowita Dormitory for about 6 months. However, this dormitory is not only for students but also for customer and traveler. The first two floors are available for people except for students. Furthermore, you will stay in a room at the hotel that closes to the bus station and city center on payment of a small fee.

Address: Zwierzyniecka 7, 60-813 Poznań, Poland

>TOURIST

42. DO YOU NEED TO RELAX?

After all that walking, it is time to rest your feet and body. How about relaxing? Thermal baths or sauna will be good for you. Malta Thermal Baths offer you a water world with countless attractions. For adrenaline junkies, there are waterslides, wild rivers, and sea waves. For those seeking relaxation, there is a number of jacuzzies, saltwater pools, whirlpools, saunas, spa and beaches with rattan chairs.

Savor the moment!

Address: Termalna 1, 61-028 Poznań, Poland

43. HAVE A GOOD TIME WITH YOU CHILDREN TOGETHER

If you travel with your children, you are probably anxious about what to do with your children and how to spend time enjoyably together. But do not have to worry about it. Because you can find a lot of suggestions and hints which help, manage that time and please your little ones.

* Maltanka Park Railway

With a 600mm wide track, along Maltańskie Lake and all the way to the Zoological Garden runs the route of one of the last narrow-gauge railways in Poland. Maltanka Park Railway is a popular destination with kids of all ages and it operates every day from the end of April till the end of September.

*Adrenaline Alpine Coaster

A 500-metre-long roller coaster filled with twisting loops (even a 360-degree twist) that hauls screaming visitors around the track at 40km per hour.

*Malta Ski

Two ski slopes, one 150 meters in length, the other over 30 meters. Hours depend heavily on the weather. There are also private lessons with an English-speaking instructor.

*Malta Ski Mini Golf

Everyone can play regardless of age and previous golfing experience.

*Toboggon Run Pepsi

Hit speeds of 50km on this summer toboggan run, a daredevil experience that twists and turns the foolish and the brave over the course of a 530-meter track.

44. THE CENTER OF CULTURE, POZNAŃ

Zamek Culture Centre was built originally as a royal residence at the turn of the 20th century by Franz Schwechten to a design ordered by Kaiser Wilhelm II, today this is one of Poland's biggest cultural institutions. Hosting over 700 events annually in its palatial halls, rooms, and courtyard, the building acts as a theatre, gallery, cinema, and concert venue. The center is well-known throughout Poland and abroad and often cooperates with other cultural institutions to host exhibitions, film screenings, plays, conferences, and educational workshops.

Address: Św. Marcin 80/82, 61-809 Poznań, Poland

45. TAKE A LOOK AT THE EVENTS ON FACEBOOK

There are a lot of events all kinds of areas in all on Facebook which can pique your interest. Before arriving Poznań, you check out the events in a day, week and month.

Tip: If you want to meet new people or make new friends, you should take a look at Social English Night with Talkersi. I have made a lot of new friends thanks to it. It welcomes you with affable and friendly people every Wednesday night in Kolejka Pub. When you arrive there, an entertaining activity starts. After ringing the bell, everyone finds someone to have a talk. When the bell is ringed every 5 minutes, everyone has to change their partner and find someone new. Thus, you get an opportunity to make new friends.

I highly recommend this event!

Address: Wielka 27/29, 61-772 Poznań, Poland

46. FESTIVALS

*Malta Festival

Malta Festival is the biggest and most famous festival that is organized by Poznań. It started out as a festival to promote street theater and street art. With time due to its popularity and great reputation the festival expanded and became one of the most influential festivals in Europe dedicated to performative art forms. An important part of the festival, a part always highly anticipated is the musical part with live concerts.

*International Ice Sculpture Festival

The Ice Sculpture Festival is an event that draws ice sculptors from all over the world wanting to present their skills. Simple blocks of ice get transformed into real artwork creating a one of its kind outdoor gallery. The ready sculptures get illuminated with colorful lights making it especially worthwhile to admire them after dark. It lasts until ice melts.

*Ethno Port Festival

Ethno Port is often referred to as a „musical harbor" for acts from around the globe that are involved in creating ethnic sounds. During the 3 amazing days in June Poznań becomes filled with the inspirational sounds and vibes form basically each part of the world.

* Dancing Poznań

Dancing Poznań is an international Dance event, during which one has the opportunity to attend numerous shows and/or workshops.

47. GET WET ON "WET MONDAY"

Ladies and gentlemen please welcome Wet Monday (Lany Poniedziałek or Smigus Dyngus). I seem to hear that you want to get soaked to the skin. Here it is both an entertaining and tiring activity.

Wet Monday takes place annually on Easter Monday in Poland where people get water thrown on them. Traditionally guys soak girls on Monday, and Tuesday is time for revenge, with girls soaking the guys. It is believed that the girl that is most wet or the one that received most amounts of water, has more chances to get married.

If you encounter an event like this, be part of this entertainment.

>TOURIST

48. NIGHT LIFE IN POZNAŃ

I seem to hear that you would like to dance the night away. I know you were tired of wandering around the city and brimmed over with history. Then let's have some fun in the clubs of Poznan which are full of fun, music, excitement, and adrenaline.

*Czekolada

I think this is the most famous club among students. That's why, you can find the best DJs, experienced and well-known Polish artists in this club. The music in the club is so loud that you may think as if you were in the center of the world and everyone in the world chafed at this noise. While your ears are about to go belly up because of noise under the earth, you notice that earth's surface is always calm and tranquil when you get out of the club. I hope I made myself clear.

Address: Wrocławska 18, 61-838 Poznań, Poland

*Pijalnia Wódki i Piwa

If you side with simplicity, this calm and sincere club or pub is just for you! Beer is as cheap as dirt in here. The first thing that I liked about this place was its concept. There is nostalgic communist-era concept here. Also, if you want to sing a song, karaoke nights take place on Mon, Tue, Thu, and Sun 20:00-02:00.

Adress: Stary Rynek 85, 61-772 Poznań, Poland
*Club Dragon

You can find a musty bar dank with sweat and atmosphere. The locale is often open until the early hours of the morning. This got it the reputation of the place in Poznań which truly closes last. Dragon is also one of the few places where live vanguard jazz can be heard played regularly.

Address: Zamkowa 3, 61-768 Poznań, Poland
   *Cuba Libre

If you like the Latin dances, you can dance salsa till the novelty wears off in this club. This place goes for detail, so much so that drinkers can even take a seat in one of those clapped-out vintage bangers you see pootling round the streets of Havana. The Fiesta Latino Fridays and Disco Latino Saturdays prove seriously popular.

Address: Wrocławska 21, 61-833 Poznań, Poland

>TOURIST

49. STROLL THROUGH THE STREETS OF POZNAŃ IN NIGHTFALL

Everyone was dead, but no corpses around. Streets were empty. There was only a breeze which caused to hurt my face. The weather was cold. Even it was so cold that I thought that it caused my imagination to freeze. Was it dream or real what I saw? I could not think anything. I could feel that my cheeks got numb every time taking a step. This cold was the same as the cold that caused my imagination to freeze. I was just ambling with my hands in my pockets. The silence of the street was covered with my rising and dropping footsteps. I have abundantly perceived the smell of history. I was dazzled by the harmony of the colors of houses in Old Market Square with the lights of street lamps. This harmony which I was fascinated along with the smiles of people has warmed the cockles of my heart in spite of the bitter cold. That was one of the moments that I wish it never ended. I think I was able to imagine now.

If you want to feel the same emotion as me, just fall into the enchanting streets of Poznan and Old Market Square's arms.

50. WHAT IS THIS PLACE GOING TO TEACH YOU?

When you travel Poznań, its history deeply saddens you and this place is going to teach you to share this sorrow. You will get new experiences or emotions when you go somewhere you do not know to get warm. You have a lot of things which you will learn from this city for better or worse. If you ask me, it is worth trying. Do not hesitate to travel, just go there and savor the moment.

Enjoy the trip!

>TOURIST

TOP REASONS TO BOOK THIS TRIP

Historical Buildings: Each of them represents the traces of World War II.

Festivals: Poznań is home to festivals, each one more beautiful than other. I think the best one is International Ice Sculpture Festival.

Foods: Especially pierogi, and pancake in Manekin.

>TOURIST

OTHER RESOURCES:

https://www.inyourpocket.com/poznan

http://www.poznan.travel/en

… BONUS BOOK

50 THINGS TO KNOW ABOUT PACKING LIGHT FOR TRAVEL

PACK THE RIGHT WAY EVERY TIME

AUTHOR: MANIDIPA BHATTACHARYYA

First Published in 2015 by Dr. Lisa Rusczyk. Copyright 2015. All Rights Reserved. No part of this publication may be reproduced, including scanning and photocopying, or distributed in any form or by any means, electronic or mechanical, or stored in a database or retrieval system without prior written permission from the publisher.

Disclaimer: The publisher has put forth an effort in preparing and arranging this book. The information provided herein by the author is provided "as is". Use this information at your own risk. The publisher is not a licensed doctor. Consult your doctor before engaging in any medical activities. The publisher and author disclaim any liabilities for any loss of profit or commercial or personal damages resulting from the information contained in this book.

Edited by Melanie Howthorne

ABOUT THE AUTHOR

Manidipa Bhattacharyya is a creative writer and editor, with an education in English literature and Linguistics. After working in the IT industry for seven long years she decided to call it quits and follow her heart instead. Manidipa has been ghost writing, editing, proof reading and doing secondary research services for many story tellers and article writers for about three years. She stays in Kolkata, India with her husband and a busy two year old. In her own time Manidipa enjoys travelling, photography and writing flash fiction.

Manidipa believes in travelling light and never carries anything that she couldn't haul herself on a trip. However, travelling with her child changed the scenario. She seemed to carry the entire world with her for the baby on the first two trips. But good sense prevailed and she is again working her way to becoming a light traveler, this time with a kid.

INTRODUCTION

*He who would travel happily
must travel light.*

-Antoine de Saint-Exupéry

Travel takes you to different places from seas and mountains to deserts and much more. In your travels you get to interact with different people and their cultures. You will, however, enjoy the sights and interact positively with these new people even more, if you are travelling light.

When you travel light your mind can be free from worry about your belongings. You do not have to spend precious vacation time waiting for your luggage to arrive after a long flight. There is be no chance of your bags going missing and the best part is that you need not pay a fee for checked baggage.

People who have mastered this art of packing light will root for you to take only one carry-on, wherever you go. However, many people can find it really hard to pack light. More so if you are travelling with children. Differentiating between "must have" and "just in case" items is the starting point. There will be ample shopping avenues at your destination which are just waiting to be explored.

This book will show you 'packing' in a new 'light' – pun intended – and help you to embrace light packing practices for all of your future travels.

Off to packing!

DEDICATION

I dedicate this book to all the travel buffs that I know, who have given me great insights into the contents of their backpacks.

THE RIGHT TRAVEL GEAR

1. CHOOSE YOUR TRAVEL GEAR CAREFULLY

While selecting your travel gear, pick items that are light weight, durable and most importantly, easy to carry. There are cases with wheels so you can drag them along – these are usually on the heavy side because of the trolley. Alternatively a backpack that you can carry comfortably on your back, or even a duffel bag that you can carry easily by hand or sling across your body are also great options. Whatever you choose, one thing to keep in mind is that the luggage itself should not weigh a ton, this will give you the flexibility to bring along one extra pair of shoes if you so desire.

>TOURIST

2. CARRY THE MINIMUM NUMBER OF BAGS

Selecting light weight luggage is not everything. You need to restrict the number of bags you carry as well. One carry-on size bag is ideal for light travel. Most carriers allow one cabin baggage plus one purse, handbag or camera bag as long as it slides under the seat in front. So technically, you can carry two items of luggage without checking them in.

3. PACK ONE EXTRA BAG

Always pack one extra empty bag along with your essential items. This could be a very light weight duffel bag or even a sturdy tote bag which takes up minimal space. In the event that you end up buying a lot of souvenirs, you already have a handy bag to stuff all that into and do not have to spend time hunting for an appropriate bag.

> *I'm very strict with my packing and have everything in its right place. I never change a rule. I hardly use anything in the hotel room. I wheel my own wardrobe in and that's it.*
>
> Charlie Watts

CLOTHES & ACCESSORIES

4. PLAN AHEAD

Figure out in advance what you plan to do on your trip. That will help you to pick that one dress you need for the occasion. If you are going to attend a wedding then you have to carry formal wear. If not, you can ditch the gown for something lighter that will be comfortable during long walks or on the beach.

5. WEAR THAT JACKET

Remember that wearing items will not add extra luggage for your air travel. So wear that bulky jacket that you plan to carry for your trip. This saves space and can also help keep you warm during the chilly flight.

6. MIX AND MATCH

Carry clothes that can be interchangeably used to reinvent your look. Find one top that goes well with a couple of pairs of pants or skirts. Use tops, shirts and jackets wisely along with other accessories like a scarf or a stole to create a new look.

7. CHOOSE YOUR FABRIC WISELY

Stuffing clothes in cramped bags definitely takes its toll which results in wrinkles. It is best to carry wrinkle free, synthetic clothes or merino tops. This will eliminate the need for that small iron you usually bring along.

8. DITCH CLOTHES PACK UNDERWEAR

Pack more underwear and socks. These are the things that will give you a fresh feel even if you do not get a chance to wear fresh clothes. Moreover these are easy to wash and can be dried inside the hotel room itself.

9. CHOOSE DARK OVER LIGHT

While picking your clothes choose dark coloured ones. They are easy to colour coordinate and can last longer before needing a wash. Accidental food spills and dirt from the road are less visible on darker clothes.

10. WEAR YOUR JEANS

Take only one pair of Jeans with you, which you should wear on the flight. Remember to pick a pair that can be worn for sightseeing trips and is equally eloquent for dinner. You can add variety by adding light weight cargoes and chinos.

11. CARRY SMART ACCESSORIES

The right accessory can give you a fresh look even with the same old dress. An intelligent neck-piece, a couple of bright scarves, stoles or a sarong can be used in a number of ways to add variety to your clothing. These light weight beauties can double up as a nursing cover, a light blanket, beach wear, a modesty cover for visiting places of worship, and also makes for an enthralling game of peek-a-boo.

12. LEARN TO FOLD YOUR GARMENTS

Seasoned travellers all swear by rolling their clothes for compact and wrinkle free packing. Bundle packing, where you roll the clothes around a central object as if tying it up, is also a popular method of compact and wrinkle free packing. Stacking folded clothes one on top of another is a big no-no as it makes creases extreme and they are difficult to get rid of without ironing.

>TOURIST

13. WASH YOUR DIRTY LAUNDRY

One of the ways to avoid carrying loads of clothes is to wash the clothes you carry. At some places you might get to use the laundry services or a Laundromat but if you are in a pinch, best solution is to wash them yourself. If that is the plan then carrying quick drying clothes is highly recommended, which most often also happen to be the wrinkle free variety.

14. LEAVE THOSE TOWELS BEHIND

Regular towels take up a lot of space, are heavy and take ages to dry out. If you are staying at hotels they will provide you with towels anyway. If you are travelling to a remote place, where the availability of towels look doubtful, carry a light weight travel towel of viscose material to do the job.

15. USE A COMPRESSION BAG

Compression bags are getting lots of recommendation now days from regular travellers. These are useful for saving space in your luggage when you have to pack bulky dresses. While packing for the return trip, get help from the hotel staff to arrange a vacuum cleaner.

FOOTWEAR

16. PUT ON YOUR HIKING BOOTS

If you have plans to go hiking or trekking during your trip, you will need those bulky hiking boots. The best way to carry them is to wear them on flight to save space and luggage weight. You can remove the boots once inside and be comfortable in your socks.

17. PICKING THE RIGHT SHOES

Shoes are often the bulkiest items, along with being the dainty if you are a female. They need care and take up a lot of space in your luggage. It is advisable therefore to pick shoes very carefully. If you plan to do a lot of walking and site seeing, then wearing a pair of comfortable walking shoes are a must. For more formal occasions you can carry durable, light weight flats which will not take up much space.

18. STUFF SHOES

If you happen to pack a pair of shoes, ensure you utilize their hollow insides. Tuck small items like rolled up socks or belts to save space. They will also be easy to find.

> TOURIST

TOILETRIES

19. STASHING TOILETRIES

Carry only absolute necessities. Airline rules dictate that for one carry-on bag, liquids and gels must be in 3.4 ounce (100ml) bottles or less, and must be packed in a one quart zip-lock bag. If you are planning to stay in a hotel, the basic things will be provided for you. It's best is to buy the rest from the local market at your destination.

20. TAKE ALONG TAMPONS

Tampons are a hard to find item in a lot of countries. Figure out how many you need and pack accordingly. For longer stays you can buy them online and have them delivered to where you are staying.

21. GET PAMPERED BEFORE YOU TRAVEL

Some avid travellers suggest getting a pedicure and manicure just the day before travelling. This not only gives you a well kept look, you also save the trouble of packing nail polish. Remember, every little bit of weight reduced adds up.

ELECTRONICS

22. LUGGING ALONG ELECTRONICS

Electronics have a large role to play in our lives today. Most of us cannot imagine our lives away from our phones, laptops or tablets. However while travelling, one must consider the amount of weight these electronics add to our luggage. Thankfully smart phones come along with all the essentials tools like a camera, email access, picture editing tools and more. They are smart to the point of eliminating the need to carry multiple gadgets. Choose a smart phone that suits all your requirements and travel with the world in your palms or pocket.

23. REDUCE THE NUMBER OF CHARGERS

If you do travel with multiple electronic devices, you will have to bear the additional burden of carrying all their chargers too. Check if a single charger can be used for multiple devices. You might also consider investing in a pocket charger. These small devices support multiple devices while keeping you charged on the go.

>TOURIST

24. TRAVEL FRIENDLY APPS

Along with smart phones come numerous apps, which are immensely helpful in our travels. You name it and you have an app for it at hand – take pictures, sharing with friends and family, torch to light dark roads, maps, checking flight/train times, find hotels and many other things. Use these smart alternatives to traditional items like books to eliminate weight and save space.

I get ideas about what's essential when packing my suitcase.

-Diane von Furstenberg

TRAVELLING WITH KIDS

25. BRING ALONG THE STROLLER

Kids might enjoy walking for a while but they soon tire out and a stroller is the just the right thing for them to rest in while you continue your tour. Strollers also double duty as a luggage carrier and shopping bag holder. Remember to pick a light weight, easy to handle brand of stroller. Better yet, find out in advance if you can rent a stroller at your destination.

26. BRING ONLY ENOUGH DIAPERS FOR YOUR TRIP

Diapers take up a lot of space and add to the weight of your luggage. Therefore it is advisable to carry just enough diapers to last through the trip and a few for afterwards, till you buy fresh stock at your destination. Unless of course you are travelling to a really remote area, in which case you have no choice but to carry the load. Otherwise diapers are something you will find pretty easily.

27. TAKE ONLY A COUPLE OF TOYS

Children are easily attracted by new things in their environment. While travelling they will find numerous 'new' objects to scrutinize and play with. Packing just one favorite toy is enough, or if there is no favorite toy leave out all of them in favor of stories or imaginary games.

28. CARRY KID FRIENDLY SNACKS

Create a small snack counter in your bag to store away quick bites for those sudden hunger pangs. Depending on the child's age this could include chocolates, raisins, dry fruits, granola bars or biscuits. Also keep a bottle of water handy for your little one.

>TOURIST

These things do not add much weight and can be adjusted in a handbag or knapsack.

29. GAMES TO CARRY

Create some travel specific, imaginary games if you have slightly grown up children, like spot the attractions. Keep a coloring book and colors handy for in-flight or hotel time. Apps on your smart phone can keep the children engaged with cartoons and story books. Older children are often entertained by games available on phones or tablets. This cuts the weight of luggage down while keeping the kids entertained.

30. LET THE KIDS CARRY THEIR LOAD

A good thing is to start early sharing of responsibilities. Let your child pick a bag of his or her choice and pack it themselves. Keep tabs on what they are stuffing in their bags by asking if they will be using that item on the trip. It could start out being just an entertainment bag initially but with growing years they will learn to sort the useful from the superfluous. Children as little as four can maneuver a small trolley suitcase like a pro- their experience in pull along toys credit. If you are worried that you may be pulling it for them, you may want to start with a backpack.

31. DECIDE ON LOCATION FOR CHILDREN TO SLEEP

While on a trip you might not always get a crib at your destination, and carrying one will make life all the more difficult. Instead call ahead to see if there are any cribs or roll out beds for children. You may even put blankets on the floor. Weave them a story about camping and they will gladly sleep without any trouble.

32. GET BABY PRODUCTS DELIVERED AT YOUR DESTINATION

If you are absolutely paranoid about not getting your favourite variety of diaper or brand of baby food, check out online stores like amazon.com for services in your destination city. You can buy things online ahead of your travel and get them delivered to your hotel upon arrival.

33. FEEDING NEEDS OF YOUR INFANTS

If you are travelling with a breastfed infant, you save the trouble of carrying bottles and bottle sanitization kits. For special food, or medications, you may need to call ahead to make sure you have a refrigerator where you are staying.

34. FEEDING NEEDS OF YOUR TODDLER

With the progression from infancy to toddler, their dietary requirements too evolve. You will have to pack some snacks for travelling time. Fresh fruits and vegetables can be purchased at your destination. Most of the cities you travel to in whichever part of the world, will have baby food products and formulas, available at the local drug-store or the supermarket.

35. PICKING CLOTHES FOR YOUR BABY

Contrary to popular belief, babies can do without many changes of clothes. At the most pack 2 outfits per day. Pack mix and match type clothes for your little one as well. Pick things which are comfortable to wear and quick to dry.

36. SELECTING SHOES FOR YOUR BABY

Like outfits, kids can make do with two pairs of comfortable shoes. If you can get some water resistant shoes it will be best. To expedite drying wet shoes, you can stuff newspaper in them then wrap them with newspaper and leave them to dry overnight.

37. KEEP ONE CHANGE OF CLOTHES HANDY

Travelling with kids can be tricky. Keep a change of clothes for the kids and mum handy in your purse or tote bag. This takes a bit of space in your hand luggage but comes extremely handy in case there are any accidents or spills.

38. LEAVE BEHIND BABY ACCESSORIES

Baby accessories like their bed, bath tub, car seat, crib etc. should be left at home. Many hotels provide a crib on request, while car seats can be borrowed from friends or rented. Babies can be given a bath in the hotel sink or even in the adult bath tub with a little bit of water. If you bring a few bath toys, they can be used in the bath, pool, and out of water. They can also be sanitized easily in the sink.

39. CARRY A SMALL LOAD OF PLASTIC BAGS

With children around there are chances of a number of soiled clothes and diapers. These plastic bags help to sort the dirt from the clean inside your big bag.

These are very light weight and come in handy to other carry stuff as well at times.

PACK WITH A PURPOSE

40. PACKING FOR BUSINESS TRIPS

One neutral-colored suit should suffice. It can be paired with different shirts, ties and accessories for different occasions. One pair of black suit pants could be worn with a matching jacket for the office or with a snazzy top for dinner.

41. PACKING FOR A CRUISE

Most cruises have formal dinners, and that formal dress usually takes up a lot of space. However you might find a tuxedo to rent. For women, a short black dress with multiple accessory options will do the trick.

42. PACKING FOR A LONG TRIP OVER DIFFERENT CLIMATES

The secret packing mantra for travel over multiple climates is layering. Layering traps air around your body creating insulation against the cold. The same light t-shirt that is comfortable in a warmer climate can be the innermost layer in a colder climate.

REDUCE SOME MORE WEIGHT

43. LEAVE PRECIOUS THINGS AT HOME

Things that you would hate to lose or get damaged leave them at home. Precious jewelry, expensive gadgets or dresses, could be anything. You will not require these on your trip. Leave them at home and spare the load on your mind.

44. SEND SOUVENIRS BY MAIL

If you have spent all your money on purchasing souvenirs, carrying them back in the same bag that you brought along would be difficult. Either pack everything in another bag and check it in the airport or get everything shipped to your home. Use an international carrier for a secure transit, but this could be more expensive than the checking fees at the airport.

45. AVOID CARRYING BOOKS

Books equal to weight. There are many reading apps which you can download on your smart phone or tab.

Plus there are gadgets like Kindle and Nook that are thinner and lighter alternatives to your regular book.

CHECK, GET, SET, CHECK AGAIN

46. STRATEGIZE BEFORE PACKING

Create a travel list and prepare all that you think you need to carry along. Keep everything on your bed or floor before packing and then think through once again – do I really need that? Any item that meets this question can be avoided. Remove whatever you don't really need and pack the rest.

47. TEST YOUR LUGGAGE

Once you have fully packed for the trip take a test trip with your luggage. Take your bags and go to town for window shopping for an hour. If you enjoy your hour long trip it is good to go, if not, go home and reduce the load some more. Repeat this test till you hit the right weight.

48. ADD A ROLL OF DUCT TAPE

You might wonder why, when this book has been talking about reducing stuff, we're suddenly asking you to pack something totally unusual. This is because when you have limited supplies, duct tape is immensely helpful for small repairs – a broken bag, leaking zip-lock bag, broken sunglasses, you name it and duct tape can fix it, temporarily.

49. LIST OF ESSENTIAL ITEMS

Even though the emphasis is on packing light, there are things which have to be carried for any trip. Here is our list of essentials:

- Passport/Visa or any other ID

- Any other paper work that might be required on a trip like permits, hotel reservation confirmations etc.

- Medicines – all your prescription medicines and emergency kit, especially if you are travelling with children

- Medical or vaccination records

- Money in foreign currency if travelling to a different country

- Tickets- Email or Message them to your phone

>TOURIST

50. MAKE THE MOST OF YOUR TRIP

Wherever you are going, whatever you hope to do we encourage you to embrace it whole-heartedly. Take in the scenery, the culture and above all, enjoy your time away from home.

On a long journey even a straw weighs heavy.

-Spanish Proverb

>TOURIST

PACKING AND PLANNING TIPS

A Week before Leaving

- Arrange for someone to take care of pets and water plants.
- Stop mail and newspaper.
- Notify Credit Card companies where you are going.
- Change your thermostat settings.
- Car inspected, oil is changed, and tires have the correct pressure.
- Passports and photo identification is up to date.
- Pay bills.
- Copy important items and download travel Apps.
- Start collecting small bills for tips.

Right Before Leaving

- Clean out refrigerator.
- Empty garbage cans.
- Lock windows.
- Make sure you have the proper identification with you.
- Bring cash for tips.
- Remember travel documents.
- Lock door behind you.
- Remember wallet.
- Unplug items in house and pack chargers.

>TOURIST

READ OTHER GREATER THAN A TOURIST BOOKS

Greater Than a Tourist San Miguel de Allende Guanajuato Mexico: 50 Travel Tips from a Local by Tom Peterson

Greater Than a Tourist – Lake George Area New York USA: 50 Travel Tips from a Local by Janine Hirschklau

Greater Than a Tourist – Monterey California United States: 50 Travel Tips from a Local by Katie Begley

Greater Than a Tourist – Chanai Crete Greece: 50 Travel Tips from a Local by Dimitra Papagrigoraki

Greater Than a Tourist – The Garden Route Western Cape Province South Africa: 50 Travel Tips from a Local by Li-Anne McGregor van Aardt

Greater Than a Tourist – Sevilla Andalusia Spain: 50 Travel Tips from a Local by Gabi Gazon

Greater Than a Tourist – Kota Bharu Kelantan Malaysia: 50 Travel Tips from a Local by Aditi Shukla

Children's Book: Charlie the Cavalier Travels the World by Lisa Rusczyk

>TOURIST

> TOURIST

Visit Greater Than a Tourist for Free Travel Tips
http://GreaterThanATourist.com

Sign up for the Greater Than a Tourist Newsletter for discount days, new books, and travel information:
http://eepurl.com/cxspyf

Follow us on Facebook for tips, images, and ideas:
https://www.facebook.com/GreaterThanATourist

Follow us on Pinterest for travel tips and ideas:
http://pinterest.com/GreaterThanATourist

Follow us on Instagram for beautiful travel images:
http://Instagram.com/GreaterThanATourist

>TOURIST

> TOURIST

Please leave your honest review of this book on Amazon and Goodreads. Please send your feedback to GreaterThanaTourist@gmail.com as we continue to improve the series. We appreciate your positive and constructive feedback. Thank you.

>TOURIST

METRIC CONVERSIONS

TEMPERATURE

110° F — — 40° C
100° F —
90° F — — 30° C
80° F —
70° F — — 20° C
60° F —
50° F — — 10° C
40° F —
32° F — — 0° C
20° F —
10° F — — -10° C
0° F —
-10° F — — -18° C
-20° F — — -30° C

To convert F to C:
Subtract 32, and then multiply by 5/9 or .5555.

To Convert C to F:
Multiply by 1.8 and then add 32.

32F = 0C

LIQUID VOLUME

To Convert:	Multiply by
U.S. Gallons to Liters	3.8
U.S. Liters to Gallons	26
Imperial Gallons to U.S. Gallons	1.2
Imperial Gallons to Liters	4.55
Liters to Imperial Gallons	22

1 Liter = .26 U.S. Gallon
1 U.S. Gallon = 3.8 Liters

DISTANCE

To convert	Multiply by
Inches to Centimeters	2.54
Centimeters to Inches	39
Feet to Meters	.3
Meters to Feet	3.28
Yards to Meters	91
Meters to Yards	1.09
Miles to Kilometers	1.61
Kilometers to Miles	.62

1 Mile = 1.6 km
1 km = .62 Miles

WEIGHT

1 Ounce = .28 Grams
1 Pound = .4555 Kilograms
1 Gram = .04 Ounce
1 Kilogram = 2.2 Pounds

>TOURIST

TRAVEL QUESTIONS

- Do you bring presents home to family or friends after a vacation?
- Do you get motion sick?
- Do you have a favorite billboard?
- Do you know what to do if there is a flat tire?
- Do you like a sun roof open?
- Do you like to eat in the car?
- Do you like to wear sun glasses in the car?
- Do you like toppings on your ice cream?
- Do you use public bathrooms?
- Did you bring your cell phone and does it have power?
- Do you have a form of identification with you?
- Have you ever been pulled over by a cop?
- Have you ever given money to a stranger on a road trip?
- Have you ever taken a road trip with animals?
- Have you ever went on a vacation alone?
- Have you ever run out of gas?

- If you could move to any place in the world, where would it be?
- If you could travel anywhere in the world, where would you travel?
- If you could travel in any vehicle, which one would it be?
- If you had three things to wish for from a magic genie, what would they be?
- If you have a driver's license, how many times did it take you to pass the test?
- What are you the most afraid of on vacation?
- What do you want to get away from the most when you are on vacation?
- What foods smells bad to you?
- What item do you bring on ever trip with you away from home?
- What makes you sleepy?
- What song would you love to hear on the radio when you're cruising on the highway?
- What travel job would you want the least?
- What will you miss most while you are away from home?
- What is something you always wanted to try?

>TOURIST

- What is the best road side attraction that you ever saw?
- What is the farthest distance you ever biked?
- What is the farthest distance you ever walked?
- What is the weirdest thing you needed to buy while on vacation?
- What is your favorite candy?
- What is your favorite color car?
- What is your favorite family vacation?
- What is your favorite food?
- What is your favorite gas station drink or food?
- What is your favorite license plate design?
- What is your favorite restaurant?
- What is your favorite smell?
- What is your favorite song?
- What is your favorite sound that nature makes?
- What is your favorite thing to bring home from a vacation?
- What is your favorite vacation with friends?
- What is your favorite way to relax?

- Where is the farthest place you ever traveled in a car?
- Where is the farthest place you ever went North, South, East and West?
- Where is your favorite place in the world?
- Who is your favorite singer?
- Who taught you how to drive?
- Who will you miss the most while you are away?
- Who if the first person you will contact when you get to your destination?
- Who brought you on your first vacation?
- Who likes to travel the most in your life?
- Would you rather be hot or cold?
- Would you rather drive above, below, or at the speed limited?
- Would you rather drive on a highway or a back road?
- Would you rather go on a train or a boat?
- Would you rather go to the beach or the woods?

>TOURIST

TRAVEL BUCKET LIST

1.

2.

3.

4.

5.

6.

7.

8.

9.

10.

>TOURIST

NOTES

Made in the USA
Monee, IL
10 February 2021